The Home–School G

Reading wit
Pre-school C

for parents and other helpers

Carol Matchett

Contents

Stepping Stones for the Foundation Stage

Schofield & Sims

1 Sharing stories

Why is sharing stories important?

Curled up in an armchair ... out in the garden ... snuggled in bed ... reading a story to your child is a rewarding and pleasurable experience for both of you. But did you know that sharing stories also helps your child to learn to read?

Children learn a great deal by copying those around them. Your child has learnt to speak by listening to you and other adults talking. He or she will learn a great deal about reading by watching and listening as you share stories together.

What do children learn through sharing stories?

Children learn many different things through sharing stories.

- They learn that reading is fun! They find that books can be interesting, funny, sad, exciting or full of facts. They are eager to join in and want to learn to read.
- They learn about words. Your child will be intrigued by how you read those black squiggly marks – and will want to know more.
- They learn that reading is about getting meaning from the book. They realise that everything you read 'makes sense' and tells you something.
- They learn about the special sound of a story being read aloud. They also learn about the special language used in stories, such as, **'Once upon a time ...'**
- They learn how books work. You will find more about this in the section **Knowing about books and print**, page 8.

Remember

Try to make time for sharing stories every day. Story time can happen at any time and in any place that suits you both. Make sure it is an enjoyable and relaxing time for both of you.

Ideas for sharing stories with your child

How to read together

- Sit so that your child can see the pages of the book and can see what you are doing.

- Use your voice to make the story come alive. Use a quiet voice for sad parts and a loud voice for exciting parts. Read some parts slowly to build up excitement and read other parts quickly to suggest speed or to surprise your audience. You might feel silly to begin with, but you will soon start to enjoy it!

- Talk about the story as you read it (see Section 2, **Talking about stories**, on pages 4 and 5).

Let's read that again

- Find a story that your child likes and re-read it a few times. Soon your child will begin to join in with favourite parts. He or she will soon begin to feel like a 'reader' too.

- Read stories with repeated patterns or phrases that recur. Pause or leave a space to encourage your child to join in with repeated words and phrases: for example, '**I'll huff and I'll p_____ …**'

Text all around you!

- Remember that there are lots of other things to read in addition to stories and other books. In a typical day, you and your child are likely to read labels, posters, signs, recipes and food packages, to name but a few. Make the best use you can of the rich language environment around you.

Brainwave

Listen to children's story tapes for ideas on improving your story-reading technique.

2 Talking about stories

Why is talking about stories important?

Language is made up of four interdependent strands: speaking, listening, reading and writing. You can use stories as a focal point for speaking and listening activities, as well as for reading.

Take time over a story. Don't race through to finish it as quickly as possible. Allow time to talk about it with your child.

- Talking about a story adds to the enjoyment. Just as you enjoy talking about your favourite films, books and television programmes, your child will enjoy sharing his or her ideas about a story.

- Talking about a story helps your child to follow what is happening. In many children's books, only part of the story is told in words; the pictures tell much more.

- Talking about stories helps us to understand them better. When you comment on a story or ask questions you are helping your child to think more carefully about it. You are helping your child to understand how stories work.

- Talking about stories helps children to learn new words – and children who know lots of words and how to use them are more likely to become good readers.

Remember

When you first read a new book, keep the story moving. Stick to a few key questions and comments. At the end of the story, go back and talk in more detail about what happened.

Some things to remember when talking about stories

Talking through the story

- Comment on what is happening. Laugh, point, show surprise and think aloud. For example: 'That was funny!', 'I liked it when ...' Encourage your child to do the same.
- Talk about what is happening in the pictures. Point out important details: for example, 'Look at the monster. What is he doing?'
- Ask 'Why' and 'How' questions as well as 'What' questions. For example, ask, 'Why did he do that?', 'How did that happen?' Questions like these develop thinking and understanding. Give your child time to think before answering them.

What happens next?

- At particularly exciting or interesting points in the story, encourage your child to predict what will happen next before you turn the page. 'What do you think is in the basket?', 'What is the bear going to do now?'
- Talk about how the story might end. Then read the ending. 'Did you guess what would happen or was it a surprise?'

Re-read, remind, re-tell

- When you re-read a familiar picture book, talk about things that you did not notice the first time you read it.
- Re-telling familiar stories in your own words is another way of talking about stories. Help your child to use the pictures in the book to tell the story.
- Help the child to link events in the story with his or her own experience. For example: 'This reminds me of ...', 'Do you remember when ...?', 'How did you feel when ...?'

Brainwave

Use toys, puppets or dressing-up clothes to help you act out the story with your child. Acting out will help you to explore the story further.

3 Language development

Why is language development important?

Children learn to read more easily if they know lots of words and understand how words are put together. Reading is about making sense of words on a page and it is easier to make sense of the words if they are already familiar.

How do children learn new words?

Children learn new words by hearing them in use. They link the new word to an object, feeling or experience. They also learn how words fit together in different ways.

How can I help develop my child's language skills?

If you want to assist in your child's language development, try to do the following.

- Talk to your child so that he or she hears lots of words and learns how they are used.
- Encourage your child to talk and try out language.
- Listen and respond to your child. Build on your child's existing language skills by helping him or her to find the right word or to put words together in a new way.
- Do not over correct! Children learn by having a go. Encourage your child to use language without worrying too much about always getting it right.

Remember

Everything you do with your child is an opportunity to introduce new words and new ways of using them. Of course, you will not have time to talk in great detail about everything you do together. So choose one activity each day in which you will focus on talking and listening.

How to encourage language development

Talk through the day

- Talk with your child about what you are doing together, what you have just done and what you are going to do next.

- Comment on activities. For example, if you and your child are cooking, you might say: **'It's quite hard to stir isn't it? I think it's too thick. Shall I add some more milk?'**

- Visit different places. Talk about what you see and do while you are there. When you get back, talk about what you did. New experiences encourage the development of new language.

- Encourage talk as part of play. Through dressing up, role-play and make believe, children can try out lots of different sorts of language.

Using language – and enjoying it to the full

- Describe things as well as naming them. For example, in the garden you could use words to describe how things move, feel, or sound.

- Help your child to put words together into sentences. For example, if he or she points and says, *'Dog!'*, you might say **'Yes, the dog is wagging his tail.'** This builds on what was said and shows what a sentence sounds like.

- Encourage your child to enjoy language. For example, encourage him or her to use favourite words or phrases from poems, rhymes and stories.

Brainwave

Use mealtimes for talking about what has happened during the day. Take it in turns to talk about something you have done. Ask questions and respond to what the child says.

4 Knowing about books and print

Why is knowing about books and print important?

Before a child can begin learning to read the words on a page, he or she needs to know what a word is. Before a child can read a book, he or she needs to know how books work.

What do children need to know before they begin to read?

Before they begin to read, children need to know some basic facts.

- Many books contain both words and pictures; it is the words that we read.
- In English, we read the words from left to right.
- We read the lines at the top of the page before reading those at the bottom.
- We usually start at the front of a book, and read until we reach the back.
- We read the left-hand page before we read the right-hand page.
- We turn the pages to continue.

How do children learn about books and print?

Children learn a lot about books by watching adults read to them. However, children also need to try these ideas out for themselves. Long before they can read, children enjoy pretending. They will sit with a book and turn the pages just as adults do. They may make up a story or retell the story in their own words. Some children even learn stories off by heart.

Remember

Through playing at reading, your child is trying out ideas about books and showing you what he or she knows about reading.

Helping your child to learn about books and print

Talking about books

- When you are sharing a story together, talk about what you are doing. For example, when you pick up a book, you might say: '**Let's find the front cover.**' Or: '**I need to open the book to the start of the story.**' Later, you might say: '**Now, we have to turn the page to see what happens next.**'
- Ask your child to help you. Let him or her turn the page for you. Ask your child to find the start of the story for you, or to show you where to begin reading.
- Use words such as '**cover**', '**front**', '**back**', '**title**'. These words may be unfamiliar at first, but young children will pick them up naturally if they hear you use them.

Talking about words

- Point to the black squiggles that we call words. Explain that it is these squiggles that you are reading. Point to words in lots of different places: for example, on signs, posters, packages, labels ...
- Run your finger under the words as you read them aloud, pointing to each one. This shows that we read English across the page – from left to right.

Playing at reading

- Encourage your child to 'play at reading'. For example, the child might 'read' a story to his or her teddy bear. Praise your child for what he or she is doing right – for example, pointing to the title on the front cover or turning the pages correctly.

Brainwave

Show your child how to write words. Write something down and then read it back, pointing to each word as you read it aloud.

5   First words

How do children learn to read their first words?

Your child enjoys listening to stories. As time passes, and with your guidance, he or she will come to know about turning the pages and will often play at 'reading a book'. Your child is beginning to take more of an interest in print.

The next step is for the child to realise that those black lines of print are made up of separate bits called words.

How can I prepare my child to learn about words?

You can help your child by doing the following.

- Show the child the words in books – and in other places.
- Use the word 'words' when you talk about what you have read.
- Point out the spaces between words.
- Point to each word as you read it aloud; but don't read the words like a robot – reading should always sound fluent and natural.

As your child begins to understand how words work, he or she will start to point to particular words and ask what they say. This is a good time for your child to learn to read his or her first words.

Where should I start?

Your child's name is a good place to start. It is an important word for your child and he or she will see it in lots of places, such as on name plaques or labels or beneath pictures or photographs. Point to your child's name as you say it. Help your child to find his or her name in a variety of places and to pick it out from amongst other names.

Once your child can recognise his or her name, you can begin introducing other words. At the same time, help your child to identify different letters and letter sounds within the words, using the notes on pages 12 to 15.

> ### Remember
> Begin with words that are important to your child: for example, 'mum' and 'dad' or the names of brothers, sisters, pets or toys.

Helping your child to read words

Words all around!

- Help your child to find the same word in lots of different places: for example, in different books, around the house, in the street, in shops.
- Point out words that you and the child see often. For example, **'bus stop'**, **'ice cream'**.
- Re-read stories a number of times. Once a story has become familiar, it is easier to look closely at the words within it. Point to the words as you read them aloud.
- Talk about the shape and length of words. Point to a word and ask, **'Is this a short little word or a very long word?'**

Look closely

- Point out some common words that appear in lots of books. For example, **'look'**, **'is'**, **'a'**, **'he'**, **'she'**. Ask your child to find the same word on another page of the book you are reading, or in another book.
- Encourage your child to notice words that look similar: for example, words that begin with the same letter as his or her first name.
- As suggested on page 9, let your child see you writing words.

Brainwave

Read books with repeating patterns, such as the **Key Word Stories** in the **Daisy Lane Home–School Readers** series. In books like these, the same common words are repeated frequently – so there are lots of opportunities for learning to recognise them.

6 Playing with sounds

Why is playing with sounds important?

Words are made up of letters. Each letter stands for a different sound. When we read, we use the sounds of individual letters or groups of letters to help build up words that we don't know. This method of reading is sometimes called '**phonics**'. Teaching children phonics is known to be one of the most important strategies in helping them learn how to read.

It is very important for young children to learn the sound/s made by each letter. However, the different letter sounds can sound very similar to a young child. The child needs to listen very carefully to hear the differences. So before learning letter sounds, children need to learn to listen carefully.

How can I help my child develop listening skills?

- Encourage your child to listen to everyday sounds. For example, he or she should recognise the distinctive sounds made by different toys, animals, machines or voices.
- Help your child to 'tune in' to the sounds of words through rhyme in songs, nursery rhymes and poems. He or she needs to recognise rhyming words and to spot when the rhyme is incorrect.
- Use stories, rhymes or jingles that include lots of words beginning with the same letter to focus on sounds at the start of words.

Remember

Learning to listen and play with the sound of words is important. Look out for books with rhymes, poems and stories that play with word and letter sounds (such as the **Sound Stories** in the **Daisy Lane Home–School Readers** series).

How to play with word and letter sounds

Listening games

- Play games where your child has to listen to sounds and guess what they are. Use lots of different sounds, such as paper bags scrunching, water splashing, metal saucepan lids clanging together, a creaking door ...

- Make a pile of toys or instruments. Encourage your child to try out different sounds. Then tell the child to cover his or her eyes. Make a sound and see if he or she can guess which instrument or toy you are using.

- Use your voice to make lots of different sounds, for example, the animal sounds in 'Old MacDonald had a farm'. Ask your child to copy you.

Rhymes, songs and jingles

- Sing rhyming songs and chant well-known nursery rhymes; perform actions or clap, stamp or skip to the rhythm.

- When reading or reciting rhymes, pause just before the rhyming word and encourage your child to say it. Alternatively, you could substitute the rhyming word for one that does *not* rhyme – and let the child correct you.

- Read or recite sentences, jingles and chants where all the words start with the same letter sound. Exaggerate the repeated sounds, for example:
  Max the **m**onster likes **m**ushrooms on his **m**armalade.

Over to you!

- Make up your own 'silly sound sentences' where all the words begin with the same letter. Some letter sounds are easier to hear than others: 's' and 'm' are good ones to start with as you can stretch them out. Children thoroughly enjoy making the sounds 'sssssssss' and 'mmmmmmmm'.

- Once your child is familiar with a few letter sounds, play 'I-Spy' together.

- Make up your own versions of rhymes, giving alternative endings or using different rhyming words.

Brainwave

Make a collection of objects whose names start with the same letter sound. For example, have a **'sss'** day and collect things whose names start with a **'sss'** sound.

7 Learning about letters

At what stage should I start to link sounds and letters?

Section 6, **Playing with sounds** (pages 12 and 13), focused on listening to sounds. This section focuses on the next step – matching the different letter sounds to the individual letter shapes.

As your child begins to take an increasing interest in print, he or she will begin to notice letters. The child might ask you about the name or sound of a particular letter. At this point, you should start showing your child how sounds and letters are linked.

Which should I teach first – the sound or the name of the letter?

Each letter has a name and a sound. It is generally best to teach children the *sound* made by the letter before the *name* of the letter. It is the *sound* of the letter that is most helpful when reading. Of course, you can teach the name of the letter as well. For example, you might show a letter 's' and say: '**This is the letter "s". It makes the sound "sssssssss".**'

Where should I begin?

Begin with one or two of the letters in your child's name. Your child might already recognise these shapes. Choose letters that are easy to distinguish, for example 's' and 'm'. As well as having distinctive sounds, 's' and 'm' also have distinctive shapes.

> **Remember**
>
> It is generally best to teach the *sound* of the letter before the name. It is also best to teach the *lower-case* letter before the capital. It is lower-case letters that children see most often in books.

How to introduce letter shapes

Letter shapes in books

- When your child can recognise and pick out the *sound* of a letter, introduce him or her to the letter *shape*.

- Point to the letter on a page of a book and say the sound made by the letter. Ask your child to find the same letter shape somewhere else on the page. Use books that focus on repeated letter sounds or show pictures of various items with names that begin with the same letter. The **Sound Stories** in the **Daisy Lane Home–School Readers** series are ideal.

- Count how many times a letter appears on the page or in the book.

Letters, letters everywhere!

- Make sure your child has lots of letters around so that he or she can look for the new letter shapes. For example, display an alphabet frieze around the child's room and encourage the child to play with alphabet jigsaws, lettered building blocks and plastic or foam letters. Multisensory experiences can reinforce children's learning.

- Play 'Odd One Out' with letter shapes. For example, put out three foam letters that are the same and one that is different. Ask your child to spot the odd one out. Start with letters that have very different shapes: for example, 's' and 'c'. Then move on to more similar shapes, for example, 'b' and 'd'.

Making and remembering letter shapes

- Show your child how to write letter shapes. Write the letter in many different sizes and using lots of different media – for example, using pen, crayon, paint, or in sand.

- As you write the letters, make the sound or talk about the shape. For example: '"c" is a **curved shape**'; '"o" is **round**'; '"s" is **squiggly**'; '"m" is like the mountains – it goes up and down!'

Brainwave

Go on a 'letter hunt'! How many times can your child see a particular letter in your home or at the supermarket?

Stepping Stones for the Foundation Stage

The activities in this book will help children along the 'Stepping Stones' towards the Early Learning Goals, set out in *Curriculum guidance for the Foundation Stage* (Qualifications and Curriculum Authority, 2000):

Language for communication

- Listen to favourite rhymes and stories with increasing attention and recall.
- Join in with repeated refrains; anticipate key events and important phrases.
- Describe main story settings, events and characters.
- Question why things happen and give explanations.
- Build up vocabulary that reflects [the child's] experiences.
- Use a widening range of words to express or elaborate ideas.

Language for thinking

- Use talk to connect ideas, explain what it happening and anticipate what might happen next.

Linking sounds and letters

- Distinguish one sound from another.
- Show awareness of rhyme and alliteration.
- Continue a rhyming string.
- Hear and say initial sounds in words and know which letters represent some of the sounds.

Reading

- Listen to and join in with stories and poems.
- Show interest in illustrations and print.
- Begin to be aware of the way stories are structured.
- Suggest how a story might end.
- Know information can be relayed in the form of print.
- Hold books the correct way up and turn pages.
- Understand the concept of a word.
- Begin to recognise some familiar words.